Behavior for Success

By Vera Lee Phillips

Behavior for Success
by Vera Lee Phillips

Printed in the United States of America

ISBN 9781612155883

www.xulonpress.com

Index

Acknowledgements

Thanks to my parents Guy and Ilex Carter who reared me in a Christian home. My father was the leader as the Bible recommends. When dad was away, mother always took us to church. Honesty and integrity were very basic to my upbringing. It is much harder for a person that doesn't have these values and hasn't accepted Jesus as their personal Savior. We all sin often. I ask for forgiveness daily for those sins I recognize and those I don't.

Being legally blind when I started this book, I needed people to read what I wrote with a sharpie and print it on my computer.

Ashley Lutz Leos typed topics as I observed people's misbehavior over a period of six years.

Jennifer Johnson typed some topics and
rearranged their order.

Sarai Ann Dromgoole typed some topics,
changed margins.

God leads guides, and provides in Jesus' name. Praise
the Lord. Remember God's answers are
yes, no, or wait.

Since I started saying this sentence several times daily
in March 2010, more and more good things keep
happening just in time (JIT lifestyle).

PERSONAL BEHAVIORS

1. <u>Addiction</u> to entertainment, music, sports, constantly seeking new entertainment and also other forms of <u>lei-sure</u> time use is a sign of discontentment with one's life and can lead to destruction.

2. Are you a backseat driver? If so, you are making the driver irritated, perhaps nervous, and exasperated. This is caused because you are determined to <u>control</u> (boss) other people. This hurts friendships and family. Do you insist that your way to do things is the only <u>right</u> way to do it? This is pure thoughtlessness on your part. Do not be thoughtless with others.

3. <u>Changes</u> (improving your language, choices of behavior, attitude) are accomplished with the help of the Holy Spirit. Ultimately, we alone are responsible to change.

4. Cheating may be in business or in moral cheating, adultery, fornication (sex before marriage).

5. Envy is a sin. We might envy someone else that has something we think should be ours or what we want.

6. Are you a professional excuse maker? Do you constantly offer excuses, instead of doing what you said you would? Why do you deliberately choose to stress yourself in this way? If you said you are giving someone money, and when he or she reminds you, all you do is offer another excuse, you are lying. Do you really feel better about yourself because you said you were giving them money? This only marks you as an inconsiderate liar. Instead, choose to change.

7. Enabler. Are you an enabler? Do you hide the fact that your spouse gets drunk or high on drugs? If so you are an enabler. People must face their problems. Denying there is a problem only delays their facing it. Do you let your adult, working, son or daughter live with you without paying their keep? Do you let them get away with being too lazy to help in the home? Do you lie to cover up someone else's mistakes? If so you are both a liar and an enabler. Ask the Holy Spirit to help you if

you are a Christian. If you haven't accepted Jesus Christ as your personal Savior, read the New Testament and talk to a preacher. People that ignore temper tantrums in a child or an adult are enabling them to repeat their behavior. People must learn there are consequences to bad behavior. To help children learn put a list of consequences on the refrigerator. Also listing chores showing who is responsible that week is helpful.

8. Everyone is a <u>failure</u>. If you take a wrong turn, that is a failure. You must make a course correction. You may only win after many failures. When you tell children they are wonderful all the time, you are cheating them. If your child is often told how pretty they are, that is the wrong thing to do. Instead, teach them "pretty is as pretty does."

9. <u>Gambling</u> by lotteries, at casinos, on the Internet, or otherwise does nothing to strengthen character.

10. Gluttony, (eating too much) is a sin most Americans admit at times. We need to ask forgiveness when we do over eat.

11. Why am I HAPPY? Because I choose to be HAPPY. If a problem occurs, I find out if it can be remedied. If I can't change it or fix it, I accept it.

12. Being inconsiderate is <u>RUDE</u>. Stubborn hardheadedness is never appreciated.

13. People can change their behavior with the help of Jesus Christ. I pray that they will.

14. <u>Messy</u> behavior affects people's opinion of us. It doesn't help us build pride in ourselves.

15. <u>Patience and consideration</u> are extremely important in dealing with other people. People that practice being impatient and inconsiderate are making it inevitable that they will fail to get along with other people. They will probably be fired from their job and/or divorced.

16. <u>Persistence</u> can be a good trait, though, if it is for helping others or you improve their emotional and physical health. When the purpose is for the love of Jesus Christ, people will not hold on to bitterness, hatred and payback when someone hurts. We mostly ask the Holy Spirit to help us forgive and to pray for this person. When we respond to someone misbehaving in the same hurtful way, we are not helping him or her to heal. We

are also not growing in the love and care Jesus wants for us. We would be deliberately choosing to ruin our own health.

17. <u>Politeness,</u> thoughtfulness, and kindness—you should always be polite, thoughtful and kind on a job. It is even more important to do this at home. You may ask why. This will bring more peace at home and on the job. Your behavior influences family and other people. The person does not have to deserve good treatment. Jesus loves us, in spite of all our faults. He loves us unconditionally. We are to love and respect our parents when they don't deserve it. Be kind to your family, friends, and bosses. Show respect to them. You may be surprised at the improvement in their behavior. Speaking about private matters in public places also makes anyone sound cheap and ill bred. Say please and thank you as a matter of habit. If you receive a gift, it is always appropriate to thank the giver.

18. <u>Respecting</u> all people is a sign of emotional maturity.

RELATIONSHIPS
WITH OTHERS

1. Loud, an unpleasant voice used to express your displeasure with family or others causes a bad reaction from everyone listening. This ANGER hurts everyone's emotional, physical, and mental health. You have endangered the digestion and mental health of yourself and everyone in hearing distance. A better way to handle your anger is to stop and think how you can voice your wish for different actions or attitude by the person you are angry with. Your spouse or teenager will respond much better to a soft voice and a reasonable suggestion. Protect the health of yourself and others.

2. Do you try to control other people? As an adult, do your parents or relatives try to control you? When you are helping others, do you control them? If someone

asks you to hand him or her something of theirs, do you refuse to do it, even if it could do them no harm? Actions like this are selfish, arrogant, and controlling. Are you always asking nosy questions of friends or relatives? Where they went, who they saw, how much they spent are questions meant to be controlling, especially when done regularly. Teenagers and adults resent such intrusions. If a relative does this to you, why do you do it to another relative? Ask Jesus to take charge of your life and change you. Yelling dirty words at family, friends, or strangers is a way of trying to control them. This causes hatred, not love. How would Jesus handle this situation? May God bless you as you change your life with the help of the Holy Spirit.

3. Duty starts early when you teach your children to help at home. A three-year-old can learn to pick up their toys, etc. Each member of the household has a responsibility for the chores at home. A written schedule on the refrigerator could be useful. People are tired at the end of the workday, but certain duties remain to be done. Sharing these makes the workload lighter. Duties on the job must be performed. Neglecting some jobs we

don't like to do is not acceptable. These habits build self-respect.

4. <u>Housekeeping</u> skills should be taught to all teenagers or young adults. Some charitable organizations might consider offering this service to those that aren't taught at home. Cooking is a skill that anyone should know the basics of; preparing vegetable and meat dishes, measuring, and some baking skills. Cleaning, sewing, mending, food safety, money, and bill paying are essentials. Parents or guardians that do not teach these skills are cheating the kids. There were two good cooks in my home that did not take the time to teach me how to cook. I chopped salads, washed all dishes, and set the table. I took Home Economics, where I learned meal planning and baking. When I married, I did not know how to cook meat or vegetables. Fortunately, my husband taught me these needed skills. My son learned at home how to cook, clean, sew, and iron. Teach; don't cheat your kids.

5. The best use of life is <u>love.</u> Love is about all relationships. How do you treat other people? Love is sustained (kept alive) by action. Do little things that please your spouse, child, or others.

6. <u>Jealousy</u> hurts the jealous person more than others. Wanting to be first in the love of parents or others may hurt us. A mother, father, grandparent, or others should not have favorites. Wanting to always be the <u>favorite</u> is not a sign of strength of self-esteem. When the apostles wanted to sit on Jesus' right hand, they clearly wanted to be his favorites. Jesus loves all of us completely. Jealousy may cause violence. Jealousy used to tell others that you are grandma's favorite is a perfect example of how resentment is caused in brothers and sisters. It teaches your children that it is okay to always want to be the favorite. This idea does not recognize the love the Holy Spirit brings us. I love all my grandchildren. I do not have a favorite. My love is large enough for all of them. Jealousy can also cause a person to want to control and possess others. Then it can reach a dangerous level. We should expect our spouse to be loyal to us, and not to be flirting with others. When we commit to marriage, we expect loyalty. Following God's laws brings happiness.

7. <u>Spoiling</u> children and adults is not a way to develop their character. Letting a child hog all the attention

creates a person that always expects to be the center of attention. Teaching them to always want to be the favorite teaches jealousy. Too many children now think that they are much better than they really are, because of over self-confidence. Giving things and money to children and adults can easily spoil them if no responsibility is placed on them. When your child gets a job, it is only fair for them to pay the cost of taking them to the job. When they have a job with 40-hour workweeks, it makes sense to charge the adult the cost of keeping them in your home. Parents that charge for utilities and food are building independence in these adults. God lends children to us for a few years. We are required to teach them to be independent.

8. Men must be the <u>head of the family</u>. This does not mean that you don't listen to your wife. Each of you is given different talents. One may be better at handling money, but the spouse must agree to the plans. Most divorces are caused by money differences. Talk this over before marriage. The father must be involved in disciplining the children. You will have better adjusted children. The Bible teaches us to cleave to the spouse.

Our parents should no longer rule our lives. The father needs to take his family to church. When the father leads, 97% of the children stay in church. When the mother takes them to church without the father, only 17% stay in church. The father should also lead the prayer time. When the father does, the family grows closer to God. The mother should lead it if the father will not.

Many men believe the good life must include wine, women, and song. Excessive drinking is against the law and God's law.

Sometimes parents do not act in a way that causes automatic respect. The Bible tells us to respect our Fathers and our Mothers. We are not to judge them for eternity, as the Lord will. They are responsible for us being alive; therefore, we are to respect them.

BEHAVIOR AT WORK

I was working at a variety store in San Marcos, Texas, while attending Southwest Texas State Teachers College in 1942. The boss said I was not needed any more. After seeing that he hired someone to take my place, I realized I had been fired. I told the man that he owed me an explanation of what I had done wrong so that I did not make the same mistake on the next job. He told me that I talked to the customers too much. He did not want casual conversation. I told him that I would talk less to the customers. I stood right there and talked myself back into the job, at 18 years old.

In the 1960's, I was teaching in a school that had no disciplinary guidelines. Two young teachers asked me to write a letter asking for guidelines for discipline. These two female teachers and one male teacher signed the letter. Before I gave it to the principal, the man told the principal about the letter. The principal talked to the two females. They asked me to remove their names. I never gave the letter to the principal, but she decided to get rid of me anyway. She sent supervisors to nit-pick the behavior of my students.

That year I had three disturbed children. One, a firebug student who set fires repeatedly in his home. His mother and grandmother wanted to get help for him. His father refused.

Another boy was disturbed enough that the Red Cross had his stepfather brought back from overseas to look after him. He stayed with a grandmother that was too sick to keep him. I asked his stepfather to get him some medical help when they moved to Fort Hood.

When the principal told me that she had decided that I would not be rehired for the next year, she had an assistant superintendent present. As I left the meeting, I said, "I will bounce back." I went to another district and spent 18 happy years there. Bosses that are difficult can be dealt with.

I had a principal when I taught school in Oklahoma that liked to sit at his desk across the hall from my classroom and watch to see if a child got out of their seat. One day, a third grade boy did get out of his seat when I was writing on the chalkboard. The principal proceeded to come in and rake the child over the coals (fuss at him). This was embarrassing. I solved this problem by simply keeping my door shut. Another day this principal came by as we were going from recess to music class. He fussed at me because I had not taken them to their room first and then to music. I took them back to their room and then I took them to music. We had a break during music class. I went to his office and asked him if he wanted us to go to the room each time on the way to music. He said yes. I could not read his mind, but we would do it the way he wanted. When I confronted him this way, he knew that I did not appreciate being called down in front of the children. The teacher that had that class the year before went home crying each day. I was not about to let him get to me that much. When I left to move to Texas, he said, "we had our ups and downs, but we made it."

A pharmacist in Tyler, Texas asked me if I was through eating at the lunch counter. I answered, "Yes, sir, I have only been here 10 minutes, but I am through."

He never did that again. We were always taught to put away an order only after we had checked the invoice. One day this pharmacist put the items on the shelf without checking them off. I signed his name and gave him the invoice. He did not comment.

Asking questions about the boss's family and showing a sincere interest will probably change their attitude.

2. Employees must always be 100% honest, on time, willing to listen politely, and always treat co-workers and bosses with respect. Snippy, smart aleck remarks are totally unacceptable. Raising your voice in an unpleasant way marks you as an inconsiderate person. This behavior will get you fired in a hurry. Never let your boss or co-workers overhear you talking this way to anyone in person or on a phone. If I caught an employee mistreating others in this way, I would fire them in a minute. People should lean on the Holy Spirit to help them change their attitudes. Listen carefully to directions. If you are unable or unwilling to follow directions, you are not a good employee.

3. Integrity in business dealings needs much improvement. Some think they must pay bribes to get business. They will prosper if they will refuse to bribe anyone. They may not get some deals, but an excellent product or service will find a market.

4. Failure to GET ALONG WITH OTHERS is a primary cause of people losing jobs.

5. Laziness is harmful to the lazy person and to the family. Some people do not go to work when they could. They don't dress for success. I put in many applications and followed up by meeting the personnel director in the office. Applying by computer only is for the impersonal.

6. Whining. Speaking in a high-pitched whining voice is irritating to many people. It is also a form of pity. The attitude of poor little me is disturbing to many. If a person complains about doing chores the way you want them to, you shouldn't reprimand in a whining voice.

CIVICS

1. Many <u>laws</u> in the United States are <u>based on the</u> <u>Bible.</u> Acceptable moral behavior in the United States is based on the Biblical teachings.

2. People have many choices of how to act (behavior).

3. Governments may require certain behavior. Dictatorial regimes can be quite harsh. Nazis and communists are very dictatorial. The U.S.A has laws against many behaviors believed to be harmful to the community. Citizens of the United States of America can change these laws by voting. People in a dictatorial type of government don't have a choice.

Why did the Founding Fathers base the <u>Constitution</u> and the laws on the Bible? They knew from experience that "good" behavior created a more peaceful and manageable society.

4. If you don't share your opinion by calling, writing, e-mailing, or faxing your representative, you are a "DO NOTHING" person. You must have an opinion on some of these issues. Please do not be a "DO NOTHING" person.

5. The U.S.A started out with the educated elite having enormous influence, because many people couldn't vote. We have changed much of this. Some U.S. Senators act as though they are better than others are. They are important. They represent a lot of people, but they are not better than a waiter or a janitor. Anyone that treats a waiter rudely thinks they are not worthwhile, unless they are lording it over someone else.

6. What can you do to help your relatives put God first, spouses second, family third, then your country? Then you can help your neighborhood. Have you joined your neighborhood association? Do you take the time to contact your city, state, and national representatives about current agendas? You might help with children's sports. Plan your time instead of just eating out, watching television, and drinking alcohol. You will feel far better about yourself.

7. <u>Freedom.</u> A. Ask Jesus to forgive you for all things you have done wrong. B. Believe Jesus was sent by God to save you from your sins (wrongdoing). C. Forgive others that have hurt you, and ask forgiveness on those people you have hurt by your words or actions. D. Jesus will send the Holy Spirit to dwell in you. E. When you have the Holy Spirit within you, you will have mental peace. God does not promise anyone there will not be troubles. There will also be wars and rumors of wars before the end of the world. There will be a one-world government. We do not need to rush this. We need to get out of the evil United Nations <u>NOW</u>. The U.N. and Communism sound good on paper. They go against human nature by trying to treat people the same when there are great differences in individuals.

FAITH

1. We can't touch Jesus' wounds like doubting Thomas. We must believe Jesus went to the grave for our sins. He arose again and sent the Holy Spirit to dwell in the hearts of believers. Horror movies show bad things. Evil is controlled in this world by the Devil (Satan). When we think about these ideas to enjoy them as entertainment, we are inviting Satan into our minds. Casting spells on people is not taught as a good activity. When we add to Biblical teachings we are on dangerous grounds. Jesus sends the Holy Spirit when we accept salvation. Both good and bad supernatural spirits may be within us. Temptations to do bad things come from the bad spirits. When people keep statues or paintings of so called gods (such as Buddha), they are inviting Satan into their minds. Believing a rabbit's foot will bring good luck is

wrong. When you receive the Holy Spirit, you will have no desire to believe in false gods.

2. **John 3:16** For God so loved the world that He gave His only begotten Son, that whoever believes in Him should not perish but have everlasting life. The Bible says that we may be forgiven if we repent and change our ways and accept Jesus Christ as our personal Savior. There is one unpardonable sin, which is blaspheme (to speak irreverently) against the Holy Spirit. (**Mark 3:28-29** Verily I say unto you, All sins shall be forgiven unto the sons of men, and blasphemies wherewith soever they shall blaspheme but he that shall blaspheme against the Holy Ghost hath never forgiveness, but is in danger of eternal damnation). (**Hebrews 10:26-27** For if we sin wilfully after that we have received the knowledge of the truth, there remaineth no more sacrifice for sins, but a certain fearful looking for of judgment and fiery indignation, which shall devour the adversaries.)

When we repent and change our ways, after we have forgiven those who hurt us, Jesus sends the Holy Spirit to comfort us and guide us. If we feel that we are unable

to forgive without help, we can admit that we are help-
less and Jesus will help us forgive.

3. No one promises life on earth will be easy. We are
promised the good life in Heaven. The peace that comes
over you with this attitude is amazing.

GENERAL ETHICS

1. <u>Belittling</u> people is unacceptable behavior.

2. <u>Calling</u> people on the job about trivial matters is a nuisance. It is bad manners and totally unnecessary. Emergency calls are quite a different matter. It makes no difference if it is a family member or an acquaintance. You are taking advantage of the person you are calling on the job. Think before you call.

3. <u>Caring</u> for others means caring for their mental, emotional, and physical wellbeing. Acting in ways that upset others is not genuinely caring.

4. When you are with someone that wants to do things differently, we should pay attention to their wishes. Protecting your property and morality is more important to some than it is to others. If they wish to take

precautions you don't want such as locking things in the car trunk, you should be considerate of their feelings.

5. <u>Listen</u>, learn, and grow.

6. <u>Loudness</u> is another behavior that is looked down upon.

7. <u>Lying</u> under oath is a serious crime and sin.

8. Celebrities or others that brag (or tell others) about illicit sin are about sinning unless they are telling to regret their wrongdoing, or teaching others what to avoid.

BEHAVIOR IN PUBLIC

1. <u>Clothing</u> choices show an influence on other people's opinions of us. People that are careless about color choices or styles do not help themselves. Whether people should judge others by their attire is beside the point. People do judge others by their appearance. It is always wise to consider other's feelings. When a person is always neat and very clean, they are more favorably perceived. Sandals are not appropriate footwear for women. Men in business say they will not hire women that are wearing sandals. These ideas must be accepted if we are to make a good impression at work. Why? Because society dictates it.

Employers pay for brains, education, honesty, and good manners.

Assumptions: Do you often express your opinion about what someone else is feeling or thinking? This can become a very bad habit. If their tone of voice does not please you, it doesn't mean they meant to offend you. Automatically taking offense may escalate bad feelings. Guessing other people's intentions can be a hurtful practice. When you assume or surmise another person's intentions, you are treading on dangerous territory. If you assume a person will not amount to anything because they are overweight and/or do not dress to suit you, you are judging by appearance.

Jesus taught us that we are to be a servant to others. When He washed the disciple's feet, He illustrated humility. We should not be too proud to do humble tasks.

Sex education should be the responsibility of parents or guardians, but they have failed for a very long time. Churches have not filled the void. Instead, the government stepped in and offered sex education without a moral basis. Following the guidelines in the Bible will lead to safe sex and much enjoyment. We are not supposed to have sex outside of marriage. People who have chosen to do so should ask Jesus Christ to forgive them.

Then they should do their best to not do it again. We can not resist temptation without help. Jesus sends the Holy Spirit to help us when we have accepted His salvation. Children should learn that sex is a wonderful gift from God that we are not supposed to misuse. People don't need to hug and kiss very much before they are ready to give it all to their lover. This choice may lead to a killing disease or pregnancy. Parents, will you <u>wake up</u> and teach good moral values?

<u>Scheduling.</u> Sharing a home requires many responsibilities. The chores should be planned so that each one knows who should do this chore. When no one takes charge of planning, chaos may result. Dishes and preparation areas need to be kept very clean. Pets in the home must be well cared for. Litter pans should not smell. Walking on littered papers is especially dangerous. When people do not keep a responsible level of cleanliness, they show disrespect for themselves as well as everyone else. Counseling may help. Marriage requires many times when you do things to please your spouse when you would rather be doing something else. Spouses require love, <u>time</u>, interest, and compassion.

Do you pay your fair share of all expenses? If not, why not? Selfishness and lack of maturity may be the cause. Most people don't like a dead beat. This can be your relative, spouse, or other. People that have not practiced these traits will find marriage very hard to adjust to. When you get up, do you fix your hair, put on clean, neat clothes and present a good appearance? When you appear in public looking sloppy and unkempt, you are inviting such problems as losing a job, or a spouse.

Society has certain rules of conduct that tell us acceptable and unacceptable behavior. Being too stubborn and selfish to accept these rules of conduct in the ways we speak, dress, and act is unacceptable to the people that care about the USA and that are concerned about our welfare.

Superiority. People that think that they are better than others are not only a pain in the neck, but they are hurting themselves. They may be smarter or have more education, but that doesn't make them superior to others.

Spending. Are you a person that feels the need to spend on new things constantly? Do you often buy clothes, furniture, or household items you don't really need? This is a weakness that can lead to divorce and all kinds of problems in your life. Counseling may help you understand why you feel so insecure without new things. This is a definite weakness that needs attention.

Politeness. Hanging up on a person that yells at you gives both of you time to cool off. Answering in a low, pleasant voice helps you stay calm.

Status symbols. Many people define themselves by what they do. A doctor, lawyer, or banker may define themselves in certain ways. A carpenter, mechanic, or soldier may define themselves in other ways. When the person loses a job, they may not be willing to accept a position of lower pay or status. This may leave the family or individual needing more money. Many military personnel have this difficulty after retirement. When the person accepts the fact that they need to start over at a lower pay and status, these people feel rather lost without their former position. Many people find it necessary to avoid drinking too much or other forms showing a lack of taking responsibility and moving forward.

Stealing is against the law and a sin.

Stubbornness and hardheadedness can be very harmful to your health and happiness.

Temptation. The Devil continues to tempt us. We may have unkind thoughts. We may get angry. Temper tantrums in adults, unless caused by disease, show a lack of commitment to Jesus. When we choose activities that weaken character, we have made an unwise choice. A small percentage of gambling taxes go to schools. This source of funding is not always reliable. When people spend money on this activity that can't really afford to gamble, they are costing their family essential food, clothing, or shelter. Every dollar of taxes on harmful activities should go toward teaching people why this hurts them and how they can change, and on law enforcement, for those breaking the laws.

Virtue. It is better to be known for your virtue rather than for your success, but no one is always virtuous.

What kind of behavior is expected at work? Be on time. Never miss work unless you are really ill. Use language that doesn't sound like gutter language. Do not curse. Do not make sexual remarks (telling about having sex with someone).

Worry never fixed any problem. Some people brag about being the family worrier. The Bible tells us not to worry. When I lost my husband, I was amazed at how little I worried. The Holy Spirit sent me peaceful acceptance. I cried a lot the first month. After that, I was calm and comfortable.

Tithing. Take God's challenge and give ten percent of your pay before taxes (first fruits). God will reward you with many blessings.

When a mistake is made, always say you are sorry, and please forgive me.

Time. Do you respect other people's time? When a person has made plans for the day and informs you as to their plans, do you insist on delaying or changing their plans? This lack of consideration for other's plans and feelings illustrates a real control addict.

Respect. Individual responsibility will not allow you to disrespect others.

Salvation. I was thirteen when I accepted Jesus Christ as my personal Savior. I understood that being saved did not mean that I would no longer sin. I could get comfort by asking for the help of the Holy Spirit. Looking back over my long life, I regret my many sins. By continuing to ask for forgiveness on a daily basis (for both those current sins I recognize, and for those sins I don't), and for strength to improve, I do improve.

Wisdom. I asked the Lord for the wisdom to know when it was time to quit driving. I became legally blind in 2000 due to macular degeneration and two medications for acid reflux. In only three months, I was legally blind. I miss the freedom of driving, but I do not worry about it. Worry makes you sick. For many years, I have told God that I would never want to be rich without the wisdom to use it wisely. I feel that giving the tithe plus other giving is very important.

The Parable of the Talents (KJV)

Matthew 25: 14

For the kingdom of heaven is as a man travelling into a far country, who called his own servants, and delivered unto them his goods.

15 And unto one he gave five talents, to another two, and to another one; to every man according to his several ability; and straightway took his journey.

16 Then he that had received the five talents went and traded with the same, and made them other five talents.

17 And likewise he that had received two, he also gained other two.

18 But he that had received one went and digged in the earth, and hid his lord's money.

19 After a long time the lord of those servants cometh, and reckoneth with them.

20 And so he that had received five talents came and brought other five talents, saying, Lord, thou deliveredst unto me five talents: behold, I have gained beside them five talents more.

21 His lord said unto him, Well done, thou good and faithful servant: thou hast been faithful over a few things, I will make thee ruler over many things: enter thou into the joy of thy lord.

22 He also that had received two talents came and said, Lord, thou deliveredst unto me two talents: behold, I have gained two other talents beside them.

23 His lord said unto him, Well done, good and faithful servant; thou hast been faithful over a few things, I will make thee ruler over many things: enter thou into the joy of thy lord.

24 Then he which had received the one talent came and said, Lord, I knew thee that thou art an hard man, reaping where thou hast not sown, and gathering where thou hast not strawed:

25 And I was afraid, and went and hid thy talent in the earth: lo, there thou hast that is thine.

26 His lord answered and said unto him, Thou wicked and slothful servant, thou knewest that I reap where I sowed not, and gather where I have not strawed:

27 Thou oughtest therefore to have put my money to the exchangers, and then at my coming I should have received mine own with usury (with interest).

28 Take therefore the talent from him, and give it unto him which hath ten talents.

29 For unto every one that hath shall be given, and he shall have abundance: but from him that hath not shall be taken away even that which he hath.

30 And cast ye the unprofitable servant into outer darkness: there shall be weeping and gnashing of teeth.

The Lord is not against rich people.

II Thessalonians 3:10-15

10 For even when we were with you, this we commanded you, that if any would not work, neither should he eat.

11 For we hear that there are some which walk among you disorderly, working not at all, but are busybodies.

12 Now them that are such we command and exhort by our Lord Jesus Christ, that with quietness they work, and eat their own bread.

13 But ye, brethren, be not weary in well doing.

14 And if any man obey not our word by this epistle, note that man, and have no company with him, that he may be ashamed.

15 Yet count him not as an enemy, but admonish him as a brother.

Churches. Churches that add to God's word have turned many people against organized religion. The majority of American citizens believe in the God of the Bible. Churches are houses of sinners (hypocrites) as are all other groups.

Responsibility. Lack of responsibility is the reason that Adam and Eve were removed from the Garden of Eden. They did not admit guilt; they blamed someone else for their sins. Adam blamed Eve. Eve blamed the snake. We are supposed to admit our own mistakes (sins). We should ask forgiveness for them.

God's answers are yes, no, or wait. The Lord leads, guides, and provides. May God Bless You.